VOCAB REHAB

How do I teach vocabulary effectively with limited time?

Marilee
SPRENGER

 Alexandria, VA USA

Website: www.ascd.org
E-mail: books@ascd.org

www.ascdarias.org

Printed in the United States of America. Cover art © 2014 by ASCD. ASCD publications present a variety of viewpoints. The views expressed or implied in this book should not be interpreted as official positions of the Association.

PAPERBACK ISBN: 978-1-4166-1874-4   ASCD product #SF114047
Also available as an e-book (see Books in Print for the ISBNs).

Library of Congress Cataloging-in-Publication Data
Sprenger, Marilee, 1949-
  Vocab rehab : how do I teach vocabulary effectively in a limited time? / Marilee Sprenger.
    pages cm
  Includes bibliographical references.
  ISBN 978-1-4166-1874-4 (pbk. : alk. paper) 1. Vocabulary—Study and teaching. I. Title.
  LB1574.5.S726 2014
  372.44—dc23
                          2013044089

21 20 19 18   3 4 5 6 7 8 9 10

VOCAB REHAB

*How do I teach vocabulary
effectively with limited time?*

Want to earn a free ASCD Arias e-book?
Your opinion counts! Please take 2–3 minutes to give
us your feedback on this publication. All survey
respondents will be entered into a drawing to
win an ASCD Arias e-book.

Please visit
www.ascd.org/ariasfeedback

Thank you!

The Value of Vocabulary

At reading time, Jesse tried to make himself as small as possible as he scrunched down in his seat. This was the worst part of the school day. Having escaped embarrassment yesterday, he knew Mrs. Sprenger would call on him today. How he wished he could make himself disappear.

It wasn't that he hated books. In fact, he loved listening to his teacher read stories in different voices. His parents were always too busy or too tired from working all day to read to him and his sisters. When the class went to the library, Jesse loved to look at books about airplanes. Although he didn't understand all of the words, he loved the pictures and hoped that someday he could be a pilot. He would be daydreaming right now about gliding through the air if he weren't consumed by a fear of making mistakes if called upon to read.

Jesse moved his head so that the head of the student in front of him blocked Mrs. Sprenger's view of him. Had he had the opportunity to read about ostriches, he would have known that the "head in the sand" technique was ludicrous (and perhaps he would know what the word ludicrous *meant!). The disappearance of a face to gaze upon was a red flag to Mrs. Sprenger, from whom the dreaded phrase soon rang out: "Jesse, it is your turn to read."*

The words hung in the air for a few moments before Jesse realized that the inevitable had happened. His time had come. He rubbed his right hand anxiously up and down his thigh, as though this action would push the words out of his mouth. With his left hand, he held the book and searched for his portion of text. His eyes glazed over as he stared at the lengthy paragraph. The voice in his head panicked: "Run out of here," it said, and, "Throw up—no, don't throw up, that would be too embarrassing." He cleared his throat and prepared for the worst.

Suddenly, Mrs. Sprenger spoke once more. "I saved this part for you, Jesse. I know you like airplanes." As Jesse's eyes scanned the paragraph, he hoped for something familiar. When he saw the word pilot, *his brain responded with curiosity and a little relief. He began:*

"The pilot was having a heart at-tack and even as the kk—the knowledge came to Brian he saw the pilot sl-sl-sl-am into the seat one more time, one more a-w-f-u-l time he sl-sl-am-med back into the seat and his rr-i-ght leg jumped, no jerked, pulling the plane to the side in a sud-den twist and his head fffell for-ward and spit (spit?) came." Jesse wanted to know more about the spit and labored through the rest of the paragraph.

When he was done, he sat back waiting to hear what the next student would read. He liked this book!

Jesse's lack of word knowledge might be partly attributed to a scarcity of reading in his home. The more children are read to and the more books they have available to them at home, the more likely it is that their vocabulary will increase (Wolfe & Nevills, 2009). There is a strong correlation between success in school (and even in life) and a robust vocabulary. By the time a child is 2 years old, he or she will have, on average, a vocabulary of between 100 and 200 words and will be able to form short phrases such as "mama sit" and "dada go" (Wolfe & Nevills, 2009). Between the ages of 2 and 3, as brain activity increases in the language areas, sentences can become longer and more complex; this period offers an incredible opportunity for increasing vocabulary through reading and speaking. By the time they reach 1st grade, most children have a vocabulary of about 6,000 words, and many add another 3,000 every year through 3rd grade (Sprenger, 2013).

The Three Tiers of Vocabulary Development

In their three-tiered model of vocabulary development, Beck, McKeown, and Kucan (2013) classify words as follows:

- **Tier 1:** These are the common, everyday words that most children enter school knowing already. Since we don't need to teach these, this is a tier without tears!
- **Tier 2:** This tier consists of words that are used across the content areas and are important for students to know and understand. Included here are process words like *analyze* and *evaluate* that students will

run into on many standardized tests and that are also used at the university level, in many careers, and in everyday life. We really want to get these words into students' long-term memory.

- **Tier 3:** This tier consists of content-specific vocabulary—the words that are often defined in textbooks or glossaries. These words are important for imparting ideas during lessons and helping to build students' background knowledge.

Direct Vocabulary Instruction

Think of your brain as a filing cabinet. If you create a file for each word you hear and continually add to it, the file will eventually be full of word information, and the cabinet drawer will become well-worn and easy to open. A word becomes a true addition to your vocabulary when it is easily accessible: the more information you have stored in a word's file, the more useful the word becomes.

There are certain words that teachers need to make sure students add to their mental filing cabinets—specifically, those that don't habitually show up in the texts that we read to our students or the books that they read for themselves. According to Marzano and Pickering (2005), we teach approximately 300 such words to our students through direct vocabulary instruction each year. Research has shown that students who receive direct vocabulary instruction in content-specific terms can raise their scores on comprehension tests from the 50th percentile rank to the 83rd (Stahl & Fairbanks, 1986).

Vocabulary Diversity

It all sounds pretty simple: students come to our classrooms with a certain number of vocabulary words, they gain more as they listen and learn through dialogue and reading, and we as teachers add a few more each week through direct instruction. We can do that; we *have been doing* that. So what's the problem? Why are students having trouble with vocabulary on tests and in their speaking and writing? I believe the answer is "vocabulary diversity."

Our classrooms are far more diverse—ethnically, linguistically, and socioeconomically—than they ever were in the past. In one oft-cited six-year study, researchers Todd Hart and Betty Risley (2003) compared the vocabularies of children from white-collar, blue-collar, and low-socio-economic-status (low-SES) families. They found a huge discrepancy among the three groups in the number of words the children were exposed to at home—a finding that helps explain the discrepancy in the children's vocabulary. Bracey (2006) reached the startling conclusion that children from middle- and upper-class families actually spoke more words than mothers from low-SES families. To further underline the discrepancy, the rate of vocabulary acquisition appears to be cumulative: children with larger vocabularies learn new words faster than those with more limited vocabularies (Hart & Risley, 2003).

The more words you know, the easier it is to draw connections with new ones—an important part of forming categories. As a student learns a new word, other words are attached to it. For example, the word *airplane* is linked to *fly*, which is related to *eagle*, which is related to *birds*, and so on; these words and others form the category of "things that fly" (Stahl & Stahl, 2012). A student who learns the word *determine* might store it alongside such related words as *decide, define, conclude,* and *choose.* Such simple categories of related words can serve as building blocks for more complex categories, thus helping to build cognitive skills. Synonyms, antonyms, and other relevant data are added to a word's file as storage continues to grow, expanding over time as we hear the word take on different nuances in different contexts.

Vocabulary and Classroom Conversations

In our ever-changing world, we try our best to relate to our students. We pay attention to the music they listen to, the websites they visit, and the latest technology they're using. Building rapport with students is an important part of helping them feel safe and welcome in the classroom. The presence of solid teacher-student rapport can contribute to academic success and motivation.

Teachers will often attempt to relate to students by conversing with them on their level, adopting many of their expressions and colloquialisms. However, research suggests that this approach is not particularly conducive to vocabulary growth. We need to "teach up" by using academic language rather than kid language. (Himmele & Himmele, 2009). Consider the following conversation between a teacher and her students:

Mrs. Wiggins: I want to keep talking about the Civil War. Who remembers the year the war began? Maria?

Maria: 1861. There are really icky pictures in the book of guys with blood all over them.

James: Yeah, but it was cool to see that there were so many dead!

Mrs. Wiggins: James, did those "cool" pictures give you any ideas about this war?

James: Those guys were kinda stupid. They didn't fight good.

Mrs. Wiggins: Who was the President of the United States that these men were fighting for? Johanna?

Johanna: I would have been a nurse and put on those neat bandages. President Lincoln made those guys fight.

Mrs. Wiggins: Who remembers the President of the Confederate States? Keenan, do you remember that dude?

Keenan: Davis? Jefferson Davis?
Mrs. Wiggins: Isn't it neat to be talking history?

"Talking history"? Who is doing all of the talking? What is being said? Brain research tells us that the person doing the most talking about content is also doing the most learning (Bowman, 2011). This conversation contains few academic vocabulary words and is not calling upon higher-level thinking. And yet, it is a kind of conversation that is quite common in classrooms.

Now let's consider an alternative version:

Mrs. Wiggins: I would like to continue our discussion of the Civil War from yesterday. What role did Abraham Lincoln play in the beginning of the war? Turn to your neighbor and review the information we discussed yesterday. [The students do as they're asked.]
Mrs. Wiggins: Now, who remembers the year the war began? Maria?
Maria: 1861. There are really icky pictures in the book of guys with blood all over them.
James: Yeah, but it was cool to see that there were so many dead!
Mrs. Wiggins: James, what do those pictures illustrate about this war?
James: Those guys were kinda stupid. They didn't fight good.
Mrs. Wiggins: Let's consider the resources that the North and the South possessed.
Keenan: The North had a lot of dudes.

Mrs. Wiggins: Those "dudes" were their army. How would having a larger army affect the outcome of the war?

Johanna: I would have been a nurse and put on those neat bandages. President Lincoln made those guys from the North fight.

Mrs. Wiggins: You mean, the men who were in the army?

Johanna: Yes, the army men. They fought under the orders of Abraham Lincoln if they were fighting for the North.

Mrs. Wiggins: Who remembers the President of the Confederate States? Keenan, do you remember his name?

Keenan: Davis? Jefferson Davis? His army wasn't as big, but the fighting was in the South, so they didn't have to walk as far.

Mrs. Wiggins: In what way was the location helpful to the Southern soldiers?

Asha: They weren't as tired for the fighting since they didn't travel so far.

Mrs. Wiggins: Let's get into our groups and make a timeline of the war as we have studied thus far.

In this case, the teacher prompts the students to start talking to one another, and by talking, they engage higher levels of thinking (Sousa & Tomlinson, 2010). By using academic vocabulary and helping her students to replace some of their "kid" language, Mrs. Wiggins is encouraging her students to use classroom-appropriate language. Add to that the opportunity they have to discuss the information with other students, and the memories of using the words become easily ingrained in long-term memory.

What the Research Says

Research today is emphasizing the following essential strategies related to vocabulary instruction.

1. Replace "kid" language with academic language in the classroom. From *The Language-Rich Classroom: A Research-Based Framework for Teaching English Language Learners,* by Himmele and Himmele (2009):

> Three 3rd grade teachers at Washington Elementary—Quirine Fischer, Krista Grimm, and Roseann Sinkosky—decided to drench their students in selected academic vocabulary from the book *The Miraculous Journey of Edward Tulane* (DiCamillo, 2006). At the end of the unit, Grimm made the following observation: "If we used it, they used it. If we talked a lot using a certain vocabulary word or we kept coming back and using it, it would show up in their journals. . . . We deliberately used big words and then consistently revisited the words we wanted them to know. . . . We repeated them in ways within the context of different activities. (pp. 30–33)

2. Read aloud to students. Students' vocabularies increase when they listen to text written at a higher level than they're used to reading (Beck et al., 2013; Fisher, Flood, Lapp, & Frey, 2004). In my book, *Teaching the Critical Vocabulary of the Common Core* (2013), I offer the following suggestions:

> Read slowly, but fluently. If you are the only person who reads aloud to [your students] it is very important that you model the fluency you want to hear from them as readers. Underline words with your voice and stop occasionally to share what you are thinking, but don't interrupt the flow of the book too much.
>
> Following the reading, ask questions. Avoid *yes* or *no* questions; dig deeper. "What was the character like? What evidence is there from the text that supports your answer? Let's revisit the text and find out." (p. 194–195)

3. Flood the classroom with words. Blachowicz, Fisher, Ogle, and Taffe (2013) suggest flooding your classroom with words related to topics being studied in the form of semantic maps, word walls, and other such tools. Be sure to differentiate between words that can be taught quickly because they are easy to remember and words that will require more intensive instruction because they relate to newer content.

Vocab Rehab: An Introduction

I often joke at my trainings, "It wasn't long ago that we had no idea the brain was related to learning." The fact is, brain research did not affect our understanding of how children learn until very late in the 20th century. Around that same time, the National Reading Panel released its landmark report, "Teaching Children to Read" (National Institute of Child Health and Human Development, 2000), which found a strong vocabulary to be one of most accurate predictors of reading comprehension. By combining brain and memory research with the reading research of the National Reading Panel, I have developed an approach to teaching vocabulary that takes into account the importance of storing vocabulary in long-term memory. This approach, which I call Vocab Rehab, is intended to form strong connections in the brain over a short period of time.

Vocab Rehab provides teachers with strategies that challenge them to recondition their approach to teaching vocabulary. If we want to engage our students, we need to embrace a new mind-set for teaching vocabulary—one that calls for exploration, discovery, and playing with words and that is informed by the latest research and successful programs in the field.

Because I know that your time is valuable, I've made all of the Vocab Rehab strategies suitable for 10-minute lessons.

The words you teach should be worth those 10 minutes. How can we know that 10 minutes will make a difference? Research shows that when students are presented with a short period of learning followed by time for processing what they've learned, they are better able to connect their learning to background knowledge (Jensen, 2005). In other words, a short lesson at the end of class time can be very effective, as the brain has time to "settle" the new learning.

As Nagy and Herman once wrote, "One should not underestimate the value of any meaningful encounter with a word even if the information gained from the one encounter is relatively small" (1987, pp. 31–32). *Any* time you spend on valuable words will be, well, valuable! Even a one-minute transition strategy can help to reinforce important vocabulary words.

Remember that your students will learn about 3,000 words this year without your direct instruction. They will learn through listening and speaking, through reading and writing, and through mirroring. Your students will repeat the words they hear from you and others around them, so make sure to make the most of class time by using vocabulary that will contribute to a bank of useful words.

Why 10 Minutes?

In the 20 years I spent as a language arts teacher, I always accepted that teaching vocabulary was my responsibility—and yet, whenever I found that time was an issue, so often it was vocabulary that I put on the back burner. In the early days, when I used a vocabulary workbook, I didn't teach vocabulary so much as I assigned it. This isn't something I'm proud of, but it was so easy just to say, "Look at the words in Chapter 2 of your vocab book and fill in the activities." Later in the week, when I could find the time, I would go over the students' work, administer a test, grade it, and move on to the next chapter. My students never really "knew" the words.

I know I'm not the only teacher who has let vocabulary fall by the wayside to focus on other things. If I had known when I was younger that 10 minutes were all it took, my students and I would have been all the better for it. Think about it: in addition to the Vocab Rehab strategies offered in this publication, you can use 10 minutes to

- Introduce a word and brainstorm a definition.
- Create a simple graphic organizer.
- Act out a word.
- Draw a picture depicting a word.
- Play a review game that includes five to seven words.
- Review the words on your word wall.
- Share synonyms and antonyms for words.
- Fill out a word page in a vocabulary notebook.
- Take attendance using a vocabulary framework (e.g., when you call a student's name, you also say a vocabulary word for which the student must provide a synonym, antonym, or definition).
- Make up a jingle or song for a vocabulary word.

Sit and watch the clock tick for 10 minutes. At what point does your mind wander or do you doze off? Ten minutes can seem like a very long time, and it *can* be—time enough to get many things accomplished. Some teachers start their class periods off with a 10-minute lesson, others use the lesson as a break near the middle of class time, and others still prefer to end the class with 10 minutes of instruction.

What Do Students Need to Know to *Really* Know a Word?

In my early days of teaching, if you had asked me what a student needed to know about a word, I would have said, "how to spell it, what it means, and how to use it in a sentence." And I would have been partly right.

How do you know if a student knows a word? Dale and O'Rourke (1986) describe four levels of word knowledge, which they characterize using the following four statements:

1. I never saw the word before.

2. I've heard of the word, but I don't know what it means.

3. I recognize the word in context, and I can tell you what it is related to.

4. I know the word well.

Word knowledge can be exhibited receptively (through reading or listening) or expressively (through speaking and writing).

Take the Pledge

I, _____, pledge that I WILL NOT

• Teach vocabulary by assigning many words at once that are unrelated to the content.

- Have students look up words in a dictionary and write down the definitions verbatim.
- Find it inappropriate for my students to have and use a word wall.
- Have students write sentences using a new vocabulary word until they have learned at least five things about the word.
- Accept short, passive sentences that do not reveal the true meaning of a word.
- Permit "kid" language in the classroom—either from my students or myself.

I, _____, pledge that I WILL

- Engage students in word study on a daily basis.
- Work with students to create definitions of words that are meaningful and memorable.
- Have students create pictures and symbols that define and describe words.
- Use academic language in my classroom and encourage other faculty members to do the same.
- Expect my students to use academic vocabulary in my classroom when speaking and writing.
- Fill my classroom with books and other media to help increase vocabulary as well as knowledge.
- Read aloud texts that are at reading levels slightly higher than my students'.
- Maintain an interactive word wall—because the more often students see and hear important words, the more often they will use them.

Although teachers often tell me that they don't have the time to teach vocabulary, they will also admit to finding time to teach content that may not be essential, but that we personally care about. Vocab Rehab can change the way you look at the teaching of vocabulary. You and your students *can* fall in love with words!

According to Marzano and Simms (2013), most teachers devote very little time to vocabulary in their classrooms. As the National Governors Association Center for Best Practices and the Council of Chief State School Officers note, "vocabulary has been neither frequent nor systematic in most schools" (2010, p. 32).

Some of the Vocab Rehab strategies require prep time; others can be done off the cuff. As you see that the strategies yield success, you'll find that putting a little time into preparing for them is worthwhile. Your students can help you with this, and you can make it easier by laminating and reusing the materials. This is especially true of general academic words that your students will find across content areas as well as in college and career settings.

Keep in mind that the brain habituates easily—novel ideas are only novel for a short time. Having said that, if your students find certain strategies particularly effective, they may ask for them again and again.

Preliminary Questions

Take a look at your daily schedule and ask yourself the following questions:

- How long are your class periods?

- How much time do you currently devote to teaching vocabulary?
- What are you teaching at the moment that, although nice to know, doesn't fall into the category of "need to know"?
- How much time can you spare to make vocabulary a daily part of your lessons?

Some Tips Before Starting

Here are some basic tips and suggestions that you can incorporate into the 10-minute strategies or otherwise use in you classroom when teaching vocabulary:

1. Introduce a word and determine its definition or description with your students. When students use their own language to describe what a word means, they are more likely to remember the definition. (Sprenger, 2005).

2. Have students draw a picture of what the word represents. For example, I have seen students illustrate the word *analyze*, which means "to break something into its component parts," by depicting a figure breaking a stick over its knees, block towers tumbling down, and unpacked Russian nesting dolls.

3. Ask students to find synonyms and antonyms for each word on a list. Synonyms are often used as definitions, so the process of finding and discussing these is crucial. Give each student a nametag that includes either the critical word or its synonym. Let students figure out which words are related and form "synonym circles." The circles can line up together or work in groups that day.

4. Compose jingles or songs for words and definitions so that they'll be more easily stored in students' automatic memories.

5. Have students create semantic maps or mind maps for some words.

6. Try offbeat techniques that activate kinesthetic learning. For example, have students write a word on the back of a cheap canvas glove; a sentence on the palm; synonyms on the thumb, pointer, and middle finger; an antonym on the ring finger; and the definition on the pinky. Vocabulary gloves can be used for independent or paired practice.

7. Act out word meanings to activate students' procedural memories.

8. Use games to review and reinforce vocabulary. For example, here are some guidelines for Vocabulary Bingo:

- Hand out bingo cards that contain definitions in the squares (ideally as many squares as there are students in the class).
- Have students ask one another if they can match words to the definitions on their bingo cards; if they can, have them sign the squares for the words that they successfully match.
- Once all squares have signatures, draw student names from a container. All students with the chosen student's signature in a square block that square off.
- When students have blocked off five squares in a row, they yell, "bingo!"

- Have the students whose names were covered in the winning row say the correct word for the definition that each signed.

9. Have students create vocabulary-word pages in a notebook. When a word appears in different contexts or content areas, students can return to that page and add new information about it. This will help them use the words more easily in writing and speaking.

10. Model the use of the words in your classroom. The more often that students hear them, the more automatic their use of those words will become.

11. Be aware of eye-accessing cues. When a student is struggling with a test question, he or she will often be looking down, which often signifies the accessing of emotion—in this case, perhaps the emotion of feeling dumb. To access information such as definitions or visual memories of words, eyes must be looking up (Payne, 2013). When you observe students looking down, stand over them and ask a question that forces them to look up, thereby being more likely to access information.

Vocab Rehab:
The 10-Minute Strategies

Here is a collection of 10-minute activities that offer fun and engaging ways for your students to learn vocabulary. (Note that 10 minutes is the minimum effective level for each; you can take more time if you need to.)

The Association Game

1. Put students in teams of four or five.

2. Hand one person in each group a slip of paper that has the same vocabulary word on it (perhaps a word from your word wall).

3. The students who received a word read it to themselves and then hide it.

4. The students who received a word take another slip of paper and write down a word that is associated with the original word.

5. The new word is passed to the next student in the group, who silently reads it, hides it, writes an associated word on a slip of paper, and passes the new word to the next person.

6. The process is repeated until the last person in the group has received a word. He or she writes down an associated word and passes it to the first student.

7. Tell the whole class what the first word was, and then go around the room and ask each team what the last word was. You'll be surprised at how different they all are! Ask each person to share his or her word. Talk about how people make different associations with words. This game reinforces the idea that we store words in our brains with other words that are connected to them.

A Variation on 10 Important Words Plus

The strategy 10 Important Words Plus, originally devised by Ruth Helen Yopp and Hallie Kay Yopp (2007), is based on principles of effective vocabulary instruction and can be used at any grade level. Though the strategy usually focuses on an analysis of big ideas, I think it's an incredible tool for determining what words students may or may not know.

1. Distribute a text and 10 sticky notes to each student.

2. Read the text aloud, with students following along. As you read, students underline 5 to 10 new or unfamiliar words.

3. Have students write each of the words that they underlined on its own sticky note.

4. Ask a student to share one of the words and post it on the wall.

5. Next, any students who have also underlined that word take their sticky notes up and place them in a column under that word.

6. Repeat steps 4 and 5 until all underlined words are on the wall. As new words appear, a bar graph is formed, with each column representing a different word.

7. Analyze the graph with students and determine which words stumped the most students—that is, which ones had the tallest columns. These become the vocabulary words to be studied. (Words that are confusing to only a few students will be studied in small groups—a great differentiation opportunity!)

Getting to the Point with PowerPoint

Create a PowerPoint presentation for a vocabulary word. This will take a minimum of four slides and a maximum of six. On the first slide, show the vocabulary word, how it's pronounced, a short definition (which you may want to arrive at with your students beforehand), and derivative forms of the word (adjective, plural, etc.). When you go over this slide with students, be certain to pronounce the word clearly and have students repeat it in unison. If it doesn't sound like the students all have the pronunciation down, ask individual students whom you know can pronounce the word correctly to say it aloud a few times, and then call on students who are having trouble with the word to repeat it. This may take a minute or two, but it is well worth the time if it means that all your students feel comfortable saying the word, as they will then feel better about using it.

On the next several slides, show the word used in sentences and questions. Feel free to include pictures or graphics to encourage conversations around the word. Brain research suggests that if we add emotion to our teaching, our students will remember it better (Willis, 2008). For example, in the case of the word *adversity,* I might use one slide to ask students, "Do you know anyone who has faced adversity in order to make a difference in the world?" or "When you face adversity, to whom do you turn?" Another slide may have a quote worth discussing, such as this one widely attributed to Malcolm X: "There is no better than adversity. Every defeat, every heartbreak, every loss, contains its own seed, its own lesson on how to improve your performance the next time." Yet another slide might have a picture or video, or perhaps a group of questions that can all be answered by the word *adversity.* The more interactive and multisensory students' experiences with words are, the likelier students are to remember them.

At your next 10-minute session, have students write their own sentences or questions using the same vocabulary word, then have them exchange and comment on one another's work. Ask your students whether the word belongs on the word wall (hint: it does!) and have a student add it.

"Just in *Times*" Word Searches

This is a great upper-grade vocabulary strategy. For ACT or SAT practice, go to the online versions of quality newspapers like the *Los Angeles Times* (www.latimes.com), the *New York Times* (www.nytimes.com), or the *Washington Post* (www.washingtonpost.com). On the home page of each site, you will find a search box; have students type one of their vocabulary words into it. Several articles are likely to appear. Have students click on each article and read how their word is used in each. This activity will help students increase their word knowledge while also keeping them abreast of current events.

What's a Lanyard?

What's a lanyard? It's a rope or cord with an object suspended on it and worn around the neck. We use them at conferences to identify participants, but some teachers are attaching vocabulary words to them! An inspired idea to be sure.

Let's say you have 25 to 30 students in your classroom. You have chosen to teach 5 to 10 words each week. Have your students wear different words around their necks each day—some the actual vocabulary words, others synonyms. Have students line up for lunch, library time, or any other activity by calling them up according to words that have a similar meaning (e.g., "Everyone wearing a word that means 'to describe', please line up").

Back It Up!

Here's a pre- or post-assessment activity teachers can use at many different grade levels. (Some teachers call it I've Got Your Back!) Begin by taping definitions of words on the backs of your students. Then give all students a word or short list of words and have them walk around the room, find the correct definitions on their classmates' backs, and copy them onto a sheet of paper or a notecard. Give the students 10 minutes or less gets them up and moving quickly. Following this activity, you may either have students keep the word sheet or card on their desks and place a check mark next to the words each time they come up during the lesson, or you can simply continue with the lesson and pay no attention to the words again until later in the day or the next day.

Freeze Frame

This strategy is sometimes called Tableau and can be used at different grade levels. The idea is to give students the opportunity to act out a word—however, because they cannot move during the activity, they must think ahead and visualize exactly what the word (or, rather, the idea behind the word) should look like.

1. Divide the students into teams of three to five, depending on your class size and the complexity of the words.

2. Give each team one of the vocabulary words you have been studying.

3. Allow three to five minutes for the students to plan a frozen pose that will demonstrate the word using all group members.

4. Students must remain frozen and quiet for 10 to 15 seconds as they demonstrate the word. Remind them that their facial expressions, placement of body parts, and ability to remain focused on one thing the entire time will add to the power of the frame.

5. Have the rest of the class guess the word. Students may even offer feedback to help the team members improve their "physical definition."

Vocabulary Paint Chips

A teacher in one of my workshops shared this strategy with us. (You can find a video of the activity here: www. teachingchannel.org/videos/build-student-vocabulary.) Paint chips are the strips of paper with different shades of paint on them that you can get at hardware stores. For this activity, students use one paint chip per vocabulary word. (The chips are usually subdivided into two to five blocks representing different shades.) At the top of each chip, students write down a vocabulary word; in each block beneath the word, students write variations of the word. For example, if the word is *describe,* students might fill out the rest of the blocks on the chip with the words *describes, described,* and *description.*

There are many possible variations on this strategy. One would be to write synonyms for the word in the different blocks; another would be to designate each block for specific information (e.g., first block, vocabulary word; second block, definition; third block, variation; fourth block, synonym; fifth block, antonym). The Teaching Channel video linked to above takes this to another level.

How to get vocabulary chips? Talk to representatives of your local paint or hardware store—they are often generous with their chips. Or design your own!

Back to the Board

For this activity, divide the class into two or more teams. One student in each team sits with his or her back to the whiteboard, on which a vocabulary word is written. The rest of the team tries to explain the word to him or her. Have the teams compete to guess the word first. An example of the strategy in action can be found here: www.youtube.com/watch?v=p7j-2xteKB4.

Vocabulary Word Pages

In a loose-leaf notebook, have students devote a whole page for each vocabulary word (see Figure 1 for an example).

The page could include the student's definition of the word, visuals, synonyms, antonyms, and a space for adding information whenever the word comes up in new contexts or subject areas. Students can keep the word pages in alphabetical order, so they are easy to find; alternatively, they could forgo the notebook and keep the pages in a Word file or online.

When You Have Less Than 10 Minutes

There will be days when 10 minutes just cannot be spared. In those cases, consider the following ultra-quick strategies for vocabulary instruction.

It's a Match!

Write five vocabulary words on the board. One by one, have each student pick up a definition that is written on construction paper or an index card and place it under the correct word, saying both the word and the definition out loud. After all of the words and definitions are matched, challenge students to write a sentence using all or most of the words.

FIGURE 1: **Vocabulary Word Page**

Name:_____

Class:_____

Word:_____

My definition: _____

_____

_____

_____

_____

Synonyms	Antonyms
Visual (Picture, Icon, Symbol of the Word)	Visual (Picture, Icon, Symbol of What the Word Is Not)

Sentences and Notes

And the Question Is . . .

When using a text with unfamiliar vocabulary words, have students write a question for which the answer is one of the words. For example, if one of the words is *clairvoyant*, the question might be, "Because she could see into the future, what did Mrs. Clark call herself?" See if students can answer their classmates' questions correctly.

Quick Draw

This fun, fast-paced strategy is a great game to play when you have a few minutes at the end of class. Before you start, have a few index cards ready with vocabulary words written on them. Have a student or two come up to the board, pick an index card, and draw a representation of the word as class members try to guess it.

Nonexample Day

Throw a Koosh ball to your students; whoever catches it must provide a nonexample of any word you point to on your word wall.

Find Someone Who . . .

Have students walk around the class with a list of vocabulary words and ask their classmates questions using the words (e.g., "Did you have an *argument* today?" "Can you give me a *metaphor* to describe a rainy day?"). Students who answer a given question can then initial the word on the questioner's list.

Write a Sentence

This one is definitely a review activity, so make sure students have mastered their words. Ask them to write a sentence using "a word that means _____." Provide the definition and give students a minute or two to write their sentences. This can be a great activity for the end of class.

A Wordy Conversation

Have students pair up, with each pair receiving one of the vocabulary words. Student A begins by using the word in a sentence, student B responds using a synonym of the word, and student A responds using an antonym. Here's an example:

> **Student A:** You are very *articulate* when you speak.
> **Student B:** I try to be very *clear* with my comments.
> **Student A:** Unlike you, I can be too *vague* sometimes.

Conclusion

Anytime a new word pops up that students need to know, consider taking a few minutes to have them discuss the word with a partner or draw a colorful picture depicting the word. In this way, unanticipated "teachable moments" can become your vocabulary lesson for the day. Still, a systematic approach will provide the most benefits, so try to include a 10-minute word lesson in your class schedule. Emphasize the importance of certain words by posting them on a word wall or selecting a "Word of the Week." Work with your colleagues to decide on what words you will all be teaching, as many Tier 2 words are used across content areas. Above all, incorporate vocabulary words into your own teaching vocabulary and challenge your students to use them in everyday conversations. Let's really begin to rehab our vocabulary teaching and close the vocabulary gap.

Acknowledgments

I am indebted to the many teachers who share their strategies at my workshops. I have learned much from each of you.

I want to thank Stefani Roth for her hard work and support of this project and Ernesto Yermoli for his editing expertise.

Special thanks go to Michael Mercer, my first principal, my friend, and my mentor.

Always, I am blessed to have my supportive husband, Scott.

To give your feedback on this publication and
be entered into a drawing for a free ASCD
Arias e-book, please visit **www.ascd.org/ariasfeedback**

ENCORE

TIPS AND TAKEAWAYS

Find your starting point. If you are responsible for helping to implement standards in your school, begin by teaching the vocabulary associated with the standards. Research suggests that up to 85 percent of standardized test scores are based on student knowledge of the standards vocabulary (Tileston, 2011). Check out your grade level and content-area standards, find the words that apply to your grade level, and pre-assess your students to see what words they need to learn.

Separate the similar. Be careful when teaching words that have similar appearances at the same time; the brain needs to let a word settle in before a new word with similar characteristics can be introduced. Consider, for example, Shore, Ray, and Goolkasian's (2013) study of 400 middle school students, which found that the students tended to confuse vocabulary words that had the same prefix even when the teachers used engaging instructional strategies.

Make learning fun. It's the key to reaching students with limited literacy backgrounds. For example, how about having word windows instead of word walls? Writing on windows is a fun prospect for most students, and erasable markers can make cleanup easy. Have students find words to display on the windows as you read to them or as they read to themselves. Tell them that a "window-worthy word" is one that is interesting to them and that may also help to make their writing more interesting. Offer a specific time of day for writing the words on the window. Take time to discuss the words and have the students add them to their vocabulary notebooks.

Integrate technology with vocabulary instruction. For example, students can look up words along with their synonyms and antonyms at sites such as Dictionary.com. At the free website Quizlet.com, students can create their own flashcards and quizzes for vocabulary words. The website also includes games to reinforce the learning.

Remember that worksheets and matching or multiple-choice quizzes aren't indicators of mastery. I find that the best way to assess students' vocabulary growth is by having them actually use the words, both verbally in class and in writing. Keeping a sticker chart with student names on it is one way to encourage word use: if a student uses a vocabulary word during class, let him or her put a sticker on the chart, then jot down the student's initials and the word used on your own recording sheet. Take note when students use vocabulary words in their writing—underline them or put a smiley face next to them. This will encourage students to use the words more often. It's a good idea to include vocabulary on your writing rubric and give students points when they use the words.

Use it or lose it. The connections our brains make when we learn something new or make changes to what we have already learned are only as strong as the number of times they are used. Practice makes permanent, and perfect practice is even better! As you change your vocabulary instruction practices, the frequency with which you undertake new approaches will ingrain them in your brain. Likewise, the more your students use new words, the likelier those words are to go into long-term permanent memory. Your 10-Minute Lesson Plan will become second nature to you and to your students if you take the time to introduce it, use it often, and reinforce its importance for furthering word knowledge.

References

Beck, I. L., McKeown, M. G., & Kucan, L. (2103). *Bringing words to life* (2nd ed.). New York: Guilford Press.

Blachowicz, C., Fisher, P., Ogle, D., & Taffe, S. (2013). *Teaching academic vocabulary K–8.* New York: Guilford Press.

Bowman, S. (2011). Using brain science to make training stick. Glenbrook, NV: Bowperson Publishing.

Bracey, G. W. (2006). Poverty's infernal mechanism. *Principal Leadership, 6*(6), 60.

Dale, E., & O'Rourke, J. (1986). *Vocabulary building.* Columbus, OH: Zaner-Bloser.

DiCamillo, K. (2006). *The miraculous journey of Edward Tulane.* Somerville, MA: Candlewick Press.

Fisher, D., Flood, J., Lapp, D., & Frey, N. (2004). Interactive read-alouds: Is there a common set of implementation practices? *The Reading Teacher, 58*(1), 8–16.

Hart, B. & Risley, T. (2003). The early catastrophe: The 30 million word gap by age 3. *American Educator, 27*(1), 4–9.

Hart, B., & Risley, T. (1995). *Meaningful differences.* Baltimore: Paul Brookes.

Himmele, P., & Himmele, W. (2009) *The language-rich classroom: A research-based framework for teaching English language learners.* Alexandria, VA: ASCD.

Jensen, E. (2005). *Teaching with the brain in mind* (2nd ed.). Alexandria, VA: ASCD.

Marzano, R. J., & Pickering. D. J. (2005). *Building academic vocabulary: Teacher's manual.* Alexandria, VA: ASCD.

Marzano, R. J., & Simms, J. A. (2013). *Vocabulary for the Common Core.* Centennial, CO: Marzano Research Laboratory.

Nagy, W. E., & Herman, P. A. (1987). Breadth and depth of vocabulary knowledge: Implications for acquisition and instruction. In M. C. McKeown & M. E. Curtis (Eds.), *The nature of vocabulary acquisition* (pp. 19–35). Hillsdale, NJ: Erlbaum.

National Governors Association Center for Best Practices & Council of Chief State School Officers. (2010). *Common Core State Standards for*

English language arts & literacy in history/social studies, science, and technical subjects, Appendix A: Research supporting key elements of the standards and glossary of key terms. Washington, DC: Authors.

Payne, R. (2013). *A framework for understanding poverty* (5th ed.). Highlands, TX: Aha Process.

Shore, R., Ray, J., & Goolkasian, P. (2013). Too close for (brain) comfort: Improving science vocabulary learning in the middle grades. *Middle School Journal 44*(5), 16–21.

Sousa, D., & Tomlinson, C. (2010). *Differentiation and the brain.* Indianapolis: Solution Tree.

Sprenger, M. (2005). *How to teach so students remember.* Alexandria, VA: ASCD.

Sprenger, M. (2013). *Teaching the critical vocabulary of the Common Core: 55 words that make or break student understanding.* Alexandria, VA: ASCD.

Stahl, S. & Fairbanks, M. (1986). The effects of vocabulary instruction. *Review of Educational Research, 56*(1), 72–110.

Stahl, K. A. D., & Stahl, S. A. (2012). Young word wizards! Fostering vocabulary development in preschool and primary education. In J. Baumann & E. Kame'enui (Eds.), *Vocabulary instruction: Research to practice* (2nd ed.). New York: Guilford Press.

Tileston, D. (2011, February). *Motivating students.* Presentation at the Learning and the Brain Conference, San Francisco, California.

Willis, J. (2008). *How your child learns best.* Chicago, IL: Sourcebooks.

Wolfe, P., & Neville, P. (2009). *Building the reading brain* (2nd ed.). Thousand Oaks, CA: Corwin Press.

Yopp, R., & Yopp, H. (2007). Ten Important Words Plus: A Strategy for Building Word Knowledge. *The Reading Teacher, 61*(2), 157–160.

Related Resources

At the time of publication, the following ASCD resources were available (ASCD stock numbers appear in parentheses). For up-to-date information about ASCD resources, go to www.ascd.org. You can search the complete archives of Educational Leadership at http://www.ascd.org/el.

ASCD Edge™
Exchange ideas and connect with other educators on the social networking site ASCD Edge at http://ascdedge.ascd.org/

Print Products
Building Academic Vocabulary: Teacher's Manual by Robert J. Marzano and Debra J. Pickering (#105153)

A Teacher's Guide to Multisensory Learning: Improving Literacy by Engaging the Senses by Lawrence Baines (#108009)

Teaching Basic and Advanced Vocabulary: A Framework for Direct Instruction by Robert J. Marzano (#309113)

Teaching the Critical Vocabulary of the Common Core: 55 Words That Make or Break Student Understanding by Marilee Sprenger (#113040)

PD Online™ Courses
Literacy Strategies: Phonemic Awareness and Vocabulary Building (#PD09OC50)

For more information: send e-mail to member@ascd.org; call 1-800-933-2723 or 703-578-9600, press 2; send a fax to 703-575-5400; or write to Information Services, ASCD, 1703 N. Beauregard St., Alexandria, VA 22311-1714 USA.

About the Author

Marilee Sprenger is a veteran teacher, education consultant, and author of the books *Teaching the Critical Vocabulary of the Common Core, Brain-based Teaching in the Digital Age, Wiring the Brain for Reading,* and *How to Teach So Students Remember.* She believes in teaching to the whole child and providing brain-compatible learning environments. She can be reached by e-mail at brainlady@gmail.com or through her website, www.brainlady.com.